SETTING THE ATMOSPHERE FOR THE DAY OF WORSHIP

Endorsements

"Whether you're starting a church or you simply want to re-evaluate your current ministry, Joe Girdler's book, *Setting the Atmosphere*, is a must read. Girdler's insights will help you to steward your God-given resources to reach people with the life-changing message of Christ. Each chapter offers the potential to move your church to the next level of ministry effectiveness."

Tom Jacobs
Superintendent, Iowa Ministry Network,
Assemblies of God

"The book *Setting the Atmosphere* by Dr. Girdler is a must read for the modern minister. Dr. Girdler is both practical and inspirational to the reader. Inspirational because when we as ministers of the gospel are given tools to go to the next level, it is inspirational! Setting the right atmosphere allows the Holy Spirit to multiply our efforts. You will be blessed and encouraged by this book."

Dr. Randy Valimont
Lead Pastor, Griffin 1st AG, Griffin, GA

"As we battle daily for victory, even on our home court, Pastor Joe's experience, vision, and passion for *Setting the Atmosphere for the Day of Worship* will empower, equip, and excite leaders with a simple and effective game plan that will result in championships for individuals, marriages, families, and communities."

Jeff Sheppard
London, KY,
ret. NBA (Atlanta Hawks, Toronto Raptors, and Italy's Benetton Treviso, Cordivari Roseto, and Wurth Roma), 2X NCAA National Champion (1996, 1998), NCAA Final Four Most Valuable Player (San Antonio, 1998), Mr. Georgia Basketball (1992), Gatorade Georgia Player of the Year (1993), University of Kentucky Wildcats guard (1993-1998)

"Effective ministry begins with the work of the Holy Spirit in both the leader and the people. However, structure and systems are designed to assist the healthy local church. My friend Joe Girdler's book is a must read. His practical insights on structure and systems will help any church leader move to the next level of impact and effectiveness."

Bill Wilson
Superintendent, Oregon Ministry Network,
Assemblies of God

"I've had the honor of knowing Pastor Joe Girdler for many years and I can say without hesitance that virtually every time I'm around him I'm left with some thought that will improve my church in a practical way. The man lives, breathes, and sleeps to help the local church thrive. *Setting the Atmosphere* is a lightning-quick read that challenged me to improve how we "do church." As a church planter, this would have been a great help before we launched."

H. L. Hussmann
Lead Pastor, Daylight Church, Louisville, KY

"*Setting the Atmosphere* is an absolutely practical book of insights for any pastor or ministry leader who desires to improve the quality of their worship experience. Read this book with an open heart and carefully evaluate your current realities as though Dr. Joe Girdler actually visited your church as a mystery shopper last weekend. Your ministry can take quantum leaps forward as your apply these helpful principles."

Terry Bailey
Superintendent, Tennessee Assemblies of God

"*Setting the Atmosphere* is a practical, wide-angle view of the local church presenting its best. Unlock the doors, check the T-stat, and you've only just begun to get ready for a church service. Joe Girdler's pastor's heart and wide experience shines through in this simple scan of the church service moment from the parking lot to the "Amen." A wise leader will not only want to make ready for guests, but also convey to the stalwart, faithful members "we really DO care about this assignment from God." This simple read may well start you on a great journey of improvement."

Larry Griswold
Executive Presbyter, Assemblies of God, Plainfield, IL

"Setting the Atmosphere equips pastors to consider desired outcomes for each aspect of Sunday services and to act with intentionality. It provides practical advice, forged from life experiences, to assist the local church to take people from where they are, and to journey with them strategically and relationally, to where they need to be in Christ. This is a "must read" as it challenges the local church to be intentional, relational, and caring and in fulfillment of Ephesians 4:11-16."

Dr. Mark Flattery
Executive Director, Network211.com

"An esteemed colleague and good friend, Dr. Joe Girdler, has written a great "how to" book for pastors covering a wide range of topics—a practical A to Z on what to do and not do—in creating a meaningful church and worship experience. This short volume is not short on valuable insights and ideas, from initial drives onto the church property to becoming fully engaged as church members. Whether new to pastoring or looking for fresh perspectives on "setting the atmosphere" at your church, you'll find this book a real game-changer for ministry leadership!"

Rich Guerra
Superintendent, SoCalifornia Network, Assemblies of God

"A practical, approachable, and direct blueprint for *setting the atmosphere.* Drawing from more than 30 years of pastoral care, this book will help both new and established ministries intentionally refine all aspects of their organizational system. A much-needed read for leaders in the local church."

Steven Girdler, MD
Department of Orthopaedic Surgery, Icahn School of Medicine at Mount Sinai, New York, NY.

"*Setting the Atmosphere for the Day of Worship* is an awesome tool for any church leader to read and put in their reference library to be looked at often and to remind them of the amazing insights it holds, especially from the perspective of a visitor. I visit a lot of churches every year and as I read this book, I thought, "Wow, what insight for every leader who wants to create an atmosphere conducive to a wonderful visit and great day of worship." I highly recommend this to every church leader."

Ken Draughon
Superintendent, Alabama District, Assemblies of God

"I read through Superintendent Joe Girdler's book *Setting the Atmosphere*. Immediately it reminded me of a book I read years ago, *Simple Things Will Make a Difference*. This book is a reminder of doing everything with excellence. I will use this book for our churches in Indiana to teach practices that are practical. This book will help people sense that our places of worship are prepared for the manifest presence of God."

Don Gifford
Superintendent, Indiana Assemblies of God

"Finally, a book that will walk the pastoral team through a step by step process of evaluating the church's effectiveness when it comes to the corporal worship experience. Joe Girdler is not just theologically prepared to write such a volume, he has experience as lead pastor of a very influential and growing congregation, and probably his best contribution is his weekly visits to churches around the world. This book is the kind of stuff that churches pay thousands of dollars for in consultant fees! Pastors and leaders, do yourself a favor, get this book! Begin immediately to make the necessary evaluations and tough decisions to change."

Bill McDonald
Founder, Unsion International Television Network, Ecuador

"Dr. Girdler offers simple, practical, and pastoral guidance that will set churches up for success. If you're looking to do an honest audit on your church's weekend experience, then this book is an excellent guide. Read it, apply it, and take your church to the next level."

JP Vick, PhD, D.Min
Doctor of Ministry Program Coordinator,
Assemblies of God Theological Seminary,
Springfield, MO

"I have known Dr. Joe Girdler literally all of my life. I saw him saved and baptized, and have witnessed his devotion to God and his faith for his entire life. His successes with church planting, growth, and leadership and mentoring church leaders are obvious and many. *Setting the Atmosphere for the Day of Worship* is a treasure trove of guidance, practical tips, direction, and a plan to achieve excellence for anyone needing to improve their church's worship experience. From the perspective of a professional project manager, I really appreciate the practicality and ease of the roadmap to achieve success. You will too."

David Girdler
Mechanical Engineer (ret.) and former Vice
President of Operations of three international
chemical and pharmaceutical organizations

"Dr. Joe Girdler offers a concise yet highly practical resource for helping local churches cultivate the kind of atmosphere that is both welcoming to newcomers and spiritually nurturing for members. The insights gained from years of study and pastoral experience provide a holistic framework from which churches can critique their vision and practices from a wide spectrum of topics related to church life and ministry. Of particular relevance are the many probing questions and reflections to help the pastor and church leader see from the perspective of the visitor. I highly recommend this book for anyone involved in Christian ministry."

David Trementozzi, PhD
Vice President, Academics, Continental Theological Seminary, Brussels, Belgium

"Joe Girdler is the master of taking the overlooked things of ministry and making them alive and vivid in the mind of the pastor. All I can say about this book is, "Practical, practical, practical...and then some!" Setting the Atmosphere is an easy read that is guaranteed to make your church's worship experience better."

Dick Hardy
Cofounder, Leaders.Church

SETTING THE ATMOSPHERE FOR THE DAY OF WORSHIP

Joseph S. Girdler

Meadow Stream
PUBLISHING

SETTING THE ATMOSPHERE FOR THE DAY OF WORSHIP

Published in Crestwood, Kentucky by **Meadow Stream Publishing.**

Scripture quotations marked (NIV) are taken from the Holy Bible, New International Version®, NIV®. Copyright © 1973, 1978, 1984, 2011 by Biblica, Inc.™ Used by permission of Zondervan. All rights reserved worldwide. www.zondervan.com The "NIV" and "New International Version" are trademarks registered in the United States Patent and Trademark Office by Biblica, Inc.™

Scripture quotations marked (NLT) are taken from the Holy Bible, New Living Translation, copyright © 1996, 2004, 2015 by Tyndale House Foundation. Used by permission of Tyndale House Publishers, Inc., Carol Stream, Illinois 60188. All rights reserved.

ISBN 978-1-7337952-0-3 paperback
ISBN 978-1-7337952-1-0 eBook

Meadow Stream
PUBLISHING

Dedication

This book is dedicated to my loving wife, Dr. Renee Vannucci Girdler, who has faithfully ministered by my side since we first accepted the pastoral and missional call for the work of Christ. We do life, family, and ministry – together. Thank you, Renee, for being with me in every new adventure!

— Joseph S. Girdler, D.Min

Table of Contents

Acknowledgements

Many have invested in my life over the years, both here in my home (USA) and abroad, and I consider each a significant partner to what has become my heart for the Church. Thank you for paving the way and for putting your touch on my life.

It is a privilege to have as friends stellar younger-generation pastors Tyler Crowder, Chase Franklin, and Ryan Franks. Tyler received his MA from Evangel University in Springfield, Missouri. Chase received his MDiv from Asbury Theological Seminary in Wilmore, Kentucky. And, Ryan received his MA from Lincoln Christian University in Lincoln, Illinois. Thank you, Tyler, Chase, and Ryan, for helping me clarify a few of my ideas for this project.

Further, I offer sincere appreciation to my editor, Catherine McGee, from the days of my doctoral journey. Having received her MS from NYU, she still remains a constant encouragement for my writings.

Thank you also to Brad and Hilton Rahme of Uberwriters Christian Ghostwriters (www.uberwriters.com) for the interior layout design, cover design, and publishing assistance.

May each of you reading this find something within these pages to strengthen your work for the Lord and inspire others in their journey with the Father. These topics are relevant, critically important, and overall, culturally and contextually functional for most all-church environs. There is nothing more spectacular than the local church. Join me in working to make every gathering a genuine encounter with the One and truly holy God of all. And may He find us—upon His imminent return—faithful to the call.

Foreword

Each week, people, volunteers, lay staff, hired staff, pastors, and more all come together around the world to experience and encounter the King of Kings and Lord of Lords through weekend worship services. Over 20% of Americans claim to be in church each Sunday, and though there may not be a single magical pill or idea that builds a church faster than the next, there are common denominators of churches that are growing and doing effective ministry more than the next. Craig Groeschel calls it the "It" factor.

Is setting the atmosphere about bright lights, a warm synth pad in the back, really attractive singers, wearing the most contemporary clothing, the media technology, phone apps, preaching from a table rather than podium, or more? It could be! It could not be. Setting the atmosphere is more about vision casting and setting a tone that is right for your church.

Setting the atmosphere is not about asking good questions, but the right questions. You have to ask yourself, what message are we as a church sending when people drive into our parking lot? What are people thinking when they are greeted and walk into our lobby? Are people being met by a friendly face or someone who looks like they could strike you at any minute?

Do you have a kids ministry that's actually a ministry? Or a 90-minute, not-quite-so-tidy daycare room full of coloring, tea parties, and a volunteer who's 15 minutes late and foreign to good hygiene? Is your worship team practicing for the first time, while picking out songs 30 minutes before service? Does the first whiff of the smells delight a person? Or, does it indicate that the building was made 80 years ago? I think we get the picture! What atmosphere are you setting?

Jesus came to earth for three reasons. One reason is to show us who the Father is and debunk misconceptions of God. A second reason is to teach us how to love people. And, a third reason is to be our substitute. Within His ministry, He showed us Truth and Grace and met people where they were. Then He challenged them to change from the inside out in order to draw closer to Him while learning how to love people! Is your church atmosphere sending that message? Remember, the local church is alive for the community, not the other way around. So, every church has to evaluate their vision, mission, cultural intelligence, demographic, and community love language. When you know these answers, your church will begin to set the tone on Sundays, which will then lead the church to set an atmosphere, and the correct atmosphere means you are intentional about the message you want to send and be received.

After serving in multiple churches, one area churches seem to struggle with the most is they are not intentional. And remember, a church is always communicating a message, thought, or idea with or without the church's permission. We live in a shallow world and if we think people should just get over our awful curb appeal and bad signage, come in and give the church a chance because they want a Jesus they know nothing about, then we are delusional. And that's on us at the end of the day.

So, why set an atmosphere for your church? Is the Holy Spirit not enough? He is! Do we need to make the good news and gospel of Jesus more attractive? We don't. Aren't people supposed to come to church based off their conviction to meet and greet one another, love one another, be a part of the church body, and further the gospel through the local church? We are!

However, we are called to be Kingdom Builders, by God's will being fulfilled through us and the local church. We are called to do what is necessary to meet people where they are, introduce them to Jesus, disciple them, and challenge them to do the same for others. Do you want to know why the Pharisees and Sadducees missed the kingdom of God? They missed it because they were caught up in their religion and were too busy being self-righteous. We have to make sure that doesn't become our story as well: too busy about what everyone must look like in church and unwilling to change to reach people.

"For the Kingdom of God is already among you."
(within you) Luke 17:21 (NLT)—addition in
parenthesis mine

We are the vessels of the Holy Spirit. We are
bringing the kingdom of God to our community!
Therefore, we must ask the right questions on how to help
people's spirits, hearts, minds, and souls quiet down to
receive what the Lord has for them each and every
Sunday, and that is why we the church must be intentional
about *setting the atmosphere* for people to worship the
almighty King.

We must remember that we live in a crazy world
full of busy schedules, social media outlets full of gossip, a
nation that is constantly divided, PTA meetings, soccer
practices, ...and you name it, we're living in it. And, in the
midst of this craziness, we are called to,

"Be still, and know that I am God!" Psalm 46:10
(NLT)

Therefore, when we meet together, the local church
could do the following in preparation for people to
encounter Jesus, even if they don't know its happening:

1. First impressions outside atmosphere
2. First impressions inside atmosphere
3. Easy, obvious, and convenient
4. Transitions and flow atmosphere

5. Stage atmosphere
6. Social media atmosphere
7. Ministry atmosphere
8. Prayer atmosphere
9. Worship atmosphere
10. Offering and giving atmosphere

Dr. Joe Girdler has presented a code of practice and an operating manual to set the atmosphere of excellence and provide an atmosphere for the Holy Spirit to reach and affect hearts and lives. Every church and church leader would be well-served to follow these practical steps to church health.

Ryan Franks
Lead Pastor, Journey Church, Brandenburg, Kentucky, and Kentucky Assemblies of God "Under 40 Ministries" (U-40) Director

Introduction

For nearly fifteen years, I've preached week-to-week in a different church and a different city each ministry engagement. I've preached in Anglo churches and multicultural churches. I've preached in English-speaking churches and in nations where there would be two live translations of my English to the audience, sentence to sentence. I've learned a few things about how churches function—what they do well, and sometimes not so well. I've picked up on some things that most guests notice, recognizing from the onset of my arrival that the local church family has no concept or consideration of what the guests have noticed or are sensing. There are few places where a book of this nature—short, concise, easy to read, and easy to implement—can be found.

Originally scripted and compiled as a general overview of various considerations of church systems for pastoral leadership development and training venues which I would lead as an annual leadership cohort, I continued beyond the training offered to find church leaders and pastors fascinated and interested in these practical guide-steps for pastoral leadership. While some found these broad topics as mainstream and standard, others found items listed they had yet to consider.

Although larger churches are usually well-structured (or so one might naturally think), well-led, and well-developed in the sense of these types of day-to-day calibrations for functionality, there remain some that are surprisingly not as established as could be anticipated. Usually, it is the church guest, the first-time attender, or the well-meaning searcher looking for a church home that finds the weaknesses and observes "the little things" that are not so little. And, to them, it matters much as to whether or not they will again attend your church or further consider it as a viable and spiritually fitting home for their search.

While the topics of this book have been used in churches of varying context, some might say this book targets most especially the rural church. Few books address practical matters for rural ministry, especially as it pertains to the practical elements we'll address in the pages ahead. I love rural churches and the callings of rural pastors. In the many nations I've had the privilege to minister, the rural (and not always, but often small) church is often the core of the local Christian community and the trusted family for believers and non-believers alike when it comes to theological standards and numerous elements of encouraging community hope. Typically rural in context, the small church is oft times challenged with having available resources, multi-element trained leadership, or even the availability for attending various training opportunities in light of the necessity of bi-vocational career requirements of their leaders, family necessities, and church budgets. These realities of today's church are further reasons for a short book of this nature to offer help and encouragement, suggestions and insights, thought-provoking ideas and "a point of consideration to start from" for God-called leaders globally.

This is not intended to be a full-scope research on any of the topics below. It is quite simply a quick-read overview designed to stimulate thought and help today's church leaders better structure their worship environment so others might find the manifest presence of God. Certainly, any one of us could prepare a myriad of supplementary themes germane and applicable to the topic. It is not penned as a comprehensive analysis on the substance matters listed or to be the insinuated guide for every church or church leader.

Contextualization is critical for both scriptural and biblical preaching ministry, as well as the development and implementation of church systems. While most of the considerations offered in this work are best understood in context to North American, traditional, often-rural environs, no doubt those functioning with a mobile, metropolitan, or missional system will likewise find usable considerations offered.

Be accountable to Christ and to your leaders and colleagues. Inquire of particular fellowship or denominational standards and protocols if you are a member or a part of an organized church. Know your audience and your ministry agenda and venue. Finally, use these suggested mindsets as simply that—proposals to aid you and your team in being the most effective and efficient possible for reaching your world for Christ.

In all truth, there is nothing you can do to work up, sing up, and shout up, or raise up the presence of God. He is powerfully sovereign and, as Scripture teaches, genuinely interested in the eternal—and the everyday—aspects of all individuals on earth. The Bible says He inhabits the praises of His people. That is what really matters, isn't it? That His presence is evident to all who worship, seek, or even casually observe as first-time guests. The importance of the Church is not designed around what we do as leaders, our projects, or our strategies. The importance of the Church is that we allow God to do His work in our lives and in the lives and hearts of all who attend for worship. Understanding that primary principle should cause us as leaders to strive in offering our best for the Lord. Excellence in all we do, as much as can be presented, is our goal so the Lord and His magnificent presence can be readily and tangibly sensed and received by all open to His work in our lives.

Let's begin.

Chapter 1
From the Moment People Arrive on the Property

Guests form opinions of your church the minute they drive by—or drive onto—your property.

- If you have a larger church, do you have engaging, welcoming parking lot attendants to greet, help people to feel comfortable, and direct and assist in parking?
- If you have a smaller church, are there enough parking spaces that a guest can comfortably get a "close to the door" spot without that "ugh" and "angst" of feeling "they don't have room for me"?
    - Do regular attendees take all the good spots up close? Consider asking your team and your

regulars to make an effort to park in the furthest locations to accommodate guests, elderly, and newcomers.

- o Is the paint faded on the parking spots, or clean and fresh? Paint it.
- o Would guest parking spots help you, just in case?
- o How about handicapped parking spots?

- According to which church growth expert you read, guests determine within the first 2 to 8 minutes as to whether or not they'll be returning.
  - o That means you have less than 10 minutes to show them what you're about.
  - o That means, if they arrive 15 minutes prior to the service, they've likely made up their mind about returning prior to the first song ever being sung and prior to you ever saying one word of your message.

> *"That means, if they arrive 15 minutes prior to the service, they've likely made up their mind about returning prior to the first song ever being sung and prior to you ever saying one word of your message."*

- Is the grass mowed?
  - o Are there flowers freshly planted?

- o Is there anything at all that says to guests driving by in the community, "I would like to try there some day!"
- If you have rain on Sunday morning and do not have an awning for people to be dropped off, consider having volunteers with umbrellas to assist people from the parking lot to the building.
- If your church has a grassy/dirt parking lot, consider putting down some gravel if your budget doesn't yet afford asphalting the surface. It will do wonders to dress up the property!
- If winter weather allows a service, it goes without saying...make sure your walkways are shoveled and salted long before the service starts! We live in a litigious society. No one wants to fall and be injured, and no church needs the potential litigation that could be incurred from good people.
- Is there an awkward dingy smell or dim lighting when you walk into the building (especially if it's an older building)? These can be costly repairs or simple fixes, but they are prime and top-of-the-list items to be resolved.

> *"Before anyone arrives— turn on worship/praise music and let it play in the parking lot to greet those who drive up."*

- Consider inexpensive outdoor speaker systems that can be wired permanently in the parking lot, connected to your equipment inside.

- When you come into the church to open the doors an HOUR early or more—before anyone arrives—turn on worship/praise music and let it play in the parking lot to greet those who drive up. It sets a stage that prepares hearts. And, it says, "Wow, these people seem to care and they seem to have it together."

- What percentage of your seating is filled or available? As with the number of minutes given before someone makes a determining decision of return on your church, similar determinations are assessed based upon comfort of seating arrangements, as well as ease of parking.

  > "I remember walking in as a guest from the busy streets of Times Square and being greeted almost immediately to determine if I were a guest and would like to be seated in conveniently offered "kept open for the purpose of guests walking in" seating in the main auditorium."

  - Consider if you're 75% full, you're full. Typically in the Western church culture, with the matriarchs of the church laying their coats and purses beside them or the men and their cases, Bibles, coats, or books taking up ample seating, when people arrive and it's not comfortable for them to find seating, they reconsider their return.

o   The same considerations apply to your church's parking arrangements. So, as is possible, provide ample and convenient parking and seating for guests, newcomers, the handicapped, veterans, and seekers. On various occasions I've visited Times Square Church in NYC. I remember walking in as a guest from the busy streets of Times Square and being greeted almost immediately to determine if I were a guest and would like to be seated in conveniently offered "kept open for the purpose of guests walking in" seating in the main auditorium. Now, that's planning ahead and being purposed for your message making its highest impact on individuals in your audience.

Chapter 2
As People Walk into the Church

- Since we considered a thought on music above, envision when you go to a mall, enter an elevator, or arrive at a theatre. There's music, ambiance.
  - When people enter the church, let them enter to a welcoming environment that
    - tells them you've prayerfully prepared for their arrival.
    - tells them you're expecting and believing they will have a meaningful and spiritual experience today in your church.

- helps them feel comfortable and at ease.
- allows them to experience a comfortable and calming, welcoming, and "I like this vibe" experience, before it's ever even begun.
- But... it has begun... They just don't know it yet.

- Often when we're on vacation or with a group, it's not uncommon that someone in the group will, upon entering, ask the waiter or waitress for directions to the washrooms. Are they clearly marked and easy to get to? It's important.
- How about signage in general?

"If you think your church has plenty of signage, reconsider. You can never have enough."

- Things that our regulars take for granted, if I'm new to the church: I don't know, and I don't want to walk in and start "looking around, over my shoulders, avoiding whomever is 'hopefully' trying to greet me, just to find whatever it is I'm trusting I see."
- If you think your church has plenty of signage, reconsider. You can never have

enough. And, if you feel you've too much signage, it's likely "just right."

- Have you considered multi-generational ministry needs? Keep in mind you should not only consider ministry to children or youth (teens), but also college age, special needs individuals, various demographic marriage options, elderly and seniors ministry cares and considerations, single adult ministries, singles again, and more.

  o I'm of the opinion special needs ministries is one of the least developed, and yet most remarkable, ministry opportunities for planters and churches that want to truly make a difference in their community. Thousands

> *"I'm of the opinion special needs ministries is one of the least developed, and yet most remarkable, ministry opportunities for planters and churches that want to truly make a difference in their community."*

within distance to your church are faced with the unique challenges of special needs loved ones, and few churches offer any ministry or welcoming and lending hand at all to their needs. Do this! It may take training and a high level of commitment, but recognize what you'll be providing for this beautiful segment of society who cannot attend church, do not attend church, or feel they are not welcomed to attend church. Think through the width of your hallways, your doorways, and your sidewalks, too. It makes a difference and says, "We care."

- o There may even be contextually unique demographics you should consider that your community and environment genuinely needs but few churches care to address.

- If a guest comes with small children, it's best to have someone to "TAKE THEM" and "WALK WITH THEM" to the children's pastor/leader and to the children's church area or nursery. Don't just point and say, "It's down that way."

- If I brought in my drink, am I comfortable to bring it into the sanctuary?
  - o How would I know that, or not?
  - o Are there "house-rules" that I'm unaware of? And, if so, who made the rules? Are they outdated? Do they need to be reconsidered in light of your vision statement to reach the lost, unbelievers, unengaged, etc.?

- Do you have education, "Sunday School" (SS), Bible study classes, or small groups? How do I know that, without asking (and if I don't pick up a bulletin, provided you have one)?

- The Tour:
  - It's not uncommon when guests visit our home that Renee or I will give them a brief and casual, comfortable, and welcoming tour. Here's the living room... Here are the bedrooms... Here's the kitchen...
    - Have you ever thought of any time a newcomer arrives, they are a newly and potentially welcomed member-to-be?
    - Have someone pre-designated to be the house-warming committee. It will be their job to see them, greet them, take them on a tour, and help them feel welcome as they get to know the place and a little about the church in the journey.
  - Is there an obvious and welcoming Connection Center? A Guest-Services Booth? It's important.
  - How about language? When a volunteer assists or the pastor speaks, is the DNA of the church being communicated by the intentional church lingo? Instead of "welcome visitors," how about "welcome guests"? A visitor, for example, highlights a brand-new and nervous person who may just be looking to blend in and not be noticed. But when you

"Have someone pre-designated to be the house-warming committee."

welcome guests, it's simply implying that if you're new, you're more than a visitor, you're a guest and, most importantly, you are invited and welcomed into our family.

- How about Security? Is it organized? Do guests feel safe? Do they recognize or know—are they aware—that there is security on the premises?
- Did you provide a shuttle service or easy-entry accessibility (especially in cases of long or encumbered walks to the entrance)?
- Do you have Food Services available? Coffee? And, if so, is it well organized and legally documented (if needed)?
- Do you have door hosts/ushers/greeters? Again, it's very important.

Chapter 3
Waiting for the Service to Begin

- Having music playing is important to set the pace, allow people to feel comfortable, and provide a spiritual environment that prepares their hearts—without them realizing it—for the worship they're about to experience.
- And remember, the time before service is crucial to meeting and connecting anyone and everyone with one another! A great insight in utilizing your volunteers to the most impact is to empower them as section captains. This will allow you to know who's been missing and why they have missed service(s). We'll address this more later.

- As a Sunday School class ends, if you have a class in the sanctuary, then have someone pre-designated to be at the sound booth to turn up the worship/praise music as the SS teacher says, "Amen."
- If people are coming into an empty sanctuary to await the service, do the same. Simply have music playing 30 minutes prior to the service.
  - When I was pastoring, I even used videos/DVDs, which worked well. One Sunday a month, it would be a video about missions showing. Another Sunday it would be a contemporary music artist singing. Another Sunday it would be a country or gospel music artist singing. Another Sunday it would be a mission video regarding ministry somewhere in the United States, the local community, or from faraway lands around the world. And, these would be timed up to a countdown clock. (I was beyond grateful for amazing volunteers who served me so well in our church sound booth! They were so vital to my team at one time, I even installed a telephone system from the platform to the sound booth so I

> *"I was beyond grateful for amazing volunteers who served me so well in our church sound booth!"*

14

could at any time during the service pick up my platform receiver and communicate immediately and directly to my team. I would encourage them to fix the typo on the screen before the next verse of the song came up, or whatever. We had fun working in tandem to do our best to shine for Jesus!)

- If you use a countdown clock, be sure you stay true to it. Start the service when the countdown hits the start-time. *See below.

- If your church culture is such that the lights are dimmed for worship, make sure they are bright enough for people to comfortably see seating, read, be able to give their offering, and find exit ways.
  - o Often this culture forgets the demographic of those who will feel it, and think it, but rarely say it: "My eyes aren't as good as my children's or grandchildren's. I wish I could see to read my Bible, the bulletin they handed me, or the note just passed to me."

- Some churches use DVDs or video segments of missions or (varying options) as their countdown clocks 10 minutes, 5 minutes, or 3 minutes prior to the start of the service.

> *"Do you have Section Greeters?"*

- Do you have Section Greeters to go around and specifically shake hands, hug necks, have conversations, welcome guests, and engage people about their children and new babies or their new jobs, or whatever?

- o If not, even small churches should consider this important aspect to connecting and engaging people.
- o I remember years ago attending a large church in Phoenix, AZ. Renee and I were seated, and at one moment early in the service that church had their version of what many might call a "meet and greet moment." The couple seated just ahead of us naturally turned around to say, "Hi." But, it didn't end with that generic, non-meaningful, "Hi." They politely and very simply acknowledged they didn't remember having met us before and asked if we were new to the church. When they found out we were, they then without hesitation invited to take us to lunch at a nearby Mexican restaurant if we'd "be willing to take just one hour to have lunch." Knowing we were going to have lunch anyway, we reluctantly said, "yes," and afterward had a wonderful time with this neat couple. They explained it was actually their ministry to meet and take newcomers to lunch each Sunday. They paid for the lunches on their own tab, not church reimbursed. It was from

their heart, and though they couldn't be involved in one of the church's many weekly events or gatherings, it was one way they could give back and actually help their pastor(s) connect with people. They loved their church, and they wanted to help others be welcomed. It was an actual organized ministry of the church, and this couple was one of many couples that did the same—each and every week.

- If you use a printed bulletin:
  - Make sure things are spelled correctly.
  - Promote upcoming events.
  - Highlight upcoming speakers.
  - Use or create the highest quality graphic.
  - Change the format occasionally to help it not be too boring and too consistently "the same" every week.
  - Consider listing a missionary of the week to pray for.
    - It's a great way to get people involved in "thinking about" missions again. And, it's a great way to raise awareness, increase prayer, and upsurge giving for missions.
  - Consider listing a family of the week to pray for.

- o Consider listing a local business of the week to pray for and engage in business.
- o Consider listing a local community church of the week to pray for; yes, that's right.

> *"The conversation of systems planning is a worthy one."*

- o Consider praying weekly for a local school.
- o And, maybe you should consider eliminating your bulletin if it actually serves little to no purpose. That's up to you, but the conversation of systems planning is a worthy one.

Chapter 4
Are My Children Safe?

- Background checks, updated no less than every two years, should be mandatory for anyone working with minors. You can't be too safe if I'm entrusting my children to you. Do the background checks. Don't miss this step. It's where you begin.
- Consider well your choices of nursery workers and children's staff, whether volunteers or paid.

> *"Do the background checks. Don't miss this step."*

  - Keep in mind, teenagers are not the optimal answer for the leaders of the ministry, the head-teachers of the class, or the ones left in charge. Their assistance to the "lead-person" is often essential, but young moms and dads, guests and regulars, want to know experienced and trained caretakers are ministering to their children during the time they are in church worship services or events.

- o Know your audience and train as possible, but recognize implications for guests, newcomers, or regulars as they observe those leading in this capacity. Perception is reality to the people who have it. Do you have teenagers working? Are they solo or assistants to the actual staff? How do parents know the difference? How about men working? Are they trusted and well-adjusted with children? Or, is it painstakingly awkward for parents who are feeling uncomfortable? Or, it could be anyone's mother or adult female, who simply is socially disengaged. The variety of scenarios that could go wrong are many but critical for the church and pastor who want to do it correctly.

> *"Perception is reality to the people who have it."*

- o Be purposed, prayerful, and have your team well-trained.

- Do you have check-in security measures in place for your children?

- Do you have a sign-in for children, or childcare?
- Are you prepared for parents' questions? For example,
    - *What if my EX-Spouse shows up and says he had worked it out for him to pick up my kids today? Is your worker just going to believe him and release my kids?*
    - *My baby had a rash when we got home from church after her time in the nursery. Why did you all not change her diaper?*
    - *If you changed diapers, did you "Tag, Date, Dbl-name sign" the diapers for accountability and for my "comfort and trust"?*
    - *Why are your children's workers teenagers? Have they any training at all?*
    - *I'm an anxious new parent. Can I have any confidence that you/they will protect and take good care of my kids?*
- Check-in security measures should be in place not just for the nursery but for kids church as well. Sometimes, kids church (5 yrs.–5th grade) has their own worship service, and if so, it should have a check-in and check-out procedure of its own. If kids are dismissed to kids church at any point during the service, consider moving to a

> *"Make your nursery a ministry."*

system where parents sign them in before service and sign them out after service is over.

- And, keep in mind, nursery is not babysitting. Make your nursery a ministry, just as important in ministry—maybe more so—as the adult class offered down the hallway. You'll be surprised what little ones learn and retain years later.

Chapter 5
Are People Mingling and Milling Around?

- Or, do they come in—right on time—and leave as soon as the service is over, without really spending any quality time in relationships?
    - What are ways you could build relationships amongst the people?
    - Within the body?
    - Among social or demographic groups?
        - Without creating or encouraging cliques?
- Have you directed, encouraged, and trained the congregation as to what their next step is following their main worship service attendance?

o Have you pointed them to free resources to help them grow spiritually and/or become networked and connected to your church family?

Chapter 6
Stewardship: Receiving Tithes and Offerings

- You can win or lose points, all in how you handle tithes and offerings.
- Some churches consider, as giving tithes and offerings are an act of worship, that it adds more meaning to have people bring their offering (if physically able) to the altar instead of passing a plate. If they are unable to come forward, you can have ushers available to come to them.
    - While some churches do this successfully, keep in mind there are people in attendance who feel uncomfortable doing that, awkward to come up front, or whatever the case may

> be. Know your audience, and make it comfortable for your guests.
>   - Other churches find discussing tithes and offerings are rarely needed at all during the worship service and simply have a tithes/offerings box in the back of the sanctuary. If your church opts for this structure, communicate your system well.

- By the way, we don't TAKE people's tithes and offerings. We RECEIVE their tithes and offerings.
  - There's a big difference to how that sounds, especially to those who are not quite sold yet on the concepts anyway.
- Is it possible that the tithes and offerings are actually worship?
  - If you believe that, then why not spend more conscious time and effort with it, during it, explaining it, teaching on it, and helping people feel comfortable through your communication of it? It is biblical.

> *"Is it possible that the tithes and offerings are actually worship?"*

- Could it help guests if we explained they didn't need to feel obligated to give if they are new to the church because we're just so glad they're here with us?

- Do you ever offer a statement about "if you're writing a check, simply write it to _____"?
  - Trust me. It helps people who need those prompts. Sheep need a shepherd, and they look to pastors to guide them. They will often go where the pastor leads. And, they'll never go where never led.
  - Whether your church does "text to give" or "old-fashioned cash and checks," make sure you communicate well what you do, how you do it, and why you do it. It matters.
- How about doing a 2-minute offering thought or devotional just before you receive the tithes and offerings?
- Does your church still have someone pray over the offering? If so, set that ambiance, just like anything else.
  - Is there music under the prayer?
  - Is the person praying loud enough and strong enough for people to hear? In a mic?
  - Is it routine and meaningless, or is it meaningful, thoughtful, and significant?

Chapter 7
Special Announcements or Presentations

- If I'm not from your church's denominational background or haven't experienced your "tradition(s)," how do you design your services to help me and my family feel welcome and not apprehensive?

> *"Pay attention to segues and transitions."*

- Pay attention to segues and transitions.

- Recognize that prayer is key and important, but be cognizant of the number of times you or leaders in the services are stopping and leading in prayer. Pray, yes, but do you need to corporately pray ten times in every service?

- Be prepared to explain everything you do and the reason(s) you do it (the what and the why) each week.
    - Expect guests and be ready for them. That includes being prepared—and having your regulars recognize—that you may be explaining things each week that many or most think is redundant or unnecessary. But, keep in mind, if it's my first service, I want and need to hear it. So, have your regulars simply accept it and get used to it so I might have the privilege of comforted assimilation.
- What is Communion? Am I allowed to participate?
    - For instance, I grew up in a denominational setting that served "closed communion." In other words, one needed to be a member of that particular church to be welcomed to participate in their communion service. Now, while that's certainly not my theological stance today nor my personal preference (I want to welcome all who are a part of Christ's family), one needs to keep in mind that guests attending come from varying ecclesiastical backgrounds and they need to know and understand your process, what's being asked of them or what's standard acceptance for these matters. They are respectful, and they don't want to do anything that would be out

of order. So, help them know what "it's okay to do" or what they should not do, as the case may be.

- What is that "tongues thing that just happened"?
  - Do you make a conscious effort to regularly explain these matters in the services as/when they are being experienced?
  - I did, when I pastored. I

> *"I made a conscious effort that anytime one of our services included something that any of my friends, neighbors, or family members would be curious about, I comfortably went to the pulpit and briefly read God's word on the subject matter."*

grew up Baptist. I went to a Methodist seminary. I have a number of friends who are Catholic, mainline, independent, non-denominational, Presbyterian, Lutheran, Nazarene, Episcopal, ... whatever. So, I made a conscious effort that anytime one of our services included something that any of my friends, neighbors, or family members would be curious about, I comfortably went to the pulpit and briefly read God's word on the subject matter.

- ○ For example, if it were a message in tongues that someone offered, I'd usually go to the Apostle Paul's writings in 1 Corinthians 14, noting especially verses 14:5, 13-15, 18, 22, 27-29, 39. You get the picture.

Chapter 8
Taking Care of Guest Speakers

- Go above and beyond when it comes to hosting
  guests. They will remember you and your church and
  the honor to Christ it conveys as you do these things
  "as unto the Lord."
- Contact their Administrative Assistant (or whoever
  can offer the information) prior to their arrival and
  find out (if possible) what favorite snacks or
  beverages they prefer. Stock a small gift basket and
  leave it in their hotel room prior to their arrival.
- While customs may vary culturally or in accordance
  with various denominational or fellowship
  standards, it is this author's experience that pastors

should always plan to give guest speakers as generous an honorarium as the church can afford.

- o See Luke 10:7; Acts 6:2; 1 Corinthians 9:9-14; Philippians 4:16-19; 2 Thessalonians 3:7-10
- Consider the offer—as needed—of transportation, hotels, meals, etc.
    - o While many times guest speakers may or may not need extras such as these, and will decline, they will still graciously appreciate your offer.
    - o At other times, it will be needed.
    - o And, consider, based on who your speaker is, that many leaders/keynote-type guest speakers are on the road many weeks/weekends of the year, so their having privacy and comfortability is necessary.
    - o While the olden days of just putting them up in the pastor's house/guest bedroom, seems personal and high-touch, it can also be less private, and for a tired speaker who's been traveling many hours, or many days, a hotel may be more appropriate.
- Consider various invitations prior to the guest's arrival (so they can plan accordingly), for instance, if the pastor or someone in the leadership team is going to host them/take them to lunch.
    - o If no one says anything, then the guest arrives wondering what the plan might be or what

the pastor's/leader's expectations might be following the service. This should be worked out in advance so the guest can be aware of whether or not he/she will be going ahead and leaving the service—getting back on the road—or if they should be waiting around after the service for the pastor or someone to take them somewhere.

- If helpful for your church, consider asking the guest to stay after speaking in the service, to include a leadership session/teaching with the church's staff/board/trustees—and spouses—as deemed necessary.
    - Guest speakers are often leaders and don't mind doing that, as long as they know in advance. Many times pastors don't ask-because they hadn't thought of it or didn't know they were allowed to ask.
    - If you do add extra teaching sessions, etc., then consider increasing the honorarium accordingly.

Chapter 9
The Worship Team

- Have they rehearsed? Are they "together" and "ready" for public ministry? Sound checks and rehearsals should be completed no less than 30 minutes prior to the service.
    - And, you'll read it elsewhere in this document also, but de-clutter the stage.

> *"Have they rehearsed? Are they "together" and "ready" for public ministry?"*

    - Do they know the words, or are they trying to learn them as they "read" on stage?
    - Always make sure the singers are louder than the band.
- Are they performers, singers, or ... worshippers?

- o It makes a difference.
- Are your singers in tune? Can they sing well? Are they God-gifted?
    - o Keep in mind church leaders should not look solely for talented singers and musicians, but for anointed worshippers.
    - o It matters.
        - Same with your musicians.
            - Are they "A" players? "B" players? "C" players?
- Their dress attire?
    - o See further thoughts (#16).
    - o Does your church have a certain standard you're wanting?
        - If so, is it genuinely in your DNA and do you know, why? Or, should your previous considerations be reconsidered in the light of reaching others for Christ (the purpose of the Church)?
- If the worship team is rehearsing on Sunday morning, be aware of how the music is impacting any Sunday School classes or other activities. Example: In a smaller building, when there may be three Sunday School classes going on right next to the sanctuary, it could get quite loud and distracting in those classes if the worship team is rehearsing!

- For the platform, staging is everything, especially in a smaller setting! If your screens are low because of a low ceiling, try not to put your worship team right next to the screens. When people are to be worshipping or looking up at the lyrics (if they don't know the words), in actuality the people are keeping their eyes on the band and not worshiping.

> *"For the platform, staging is everything, especially in a smaller setting!"*

- Also for platforms, if you don't have any consistent dramas and/or if the pastor consistently preaches from the floor, consider getting rid of the platform altogether. No need to elevate just the band!
- *Consider music stands a necessary evil. Many people have been playing music for over twenty years and may still have a hard time memorizing.
- If space allows, have some type of monitor hanging in the back so the worship team can see what words the congregation sees. It can solve many cases of out-of-sync lyrics!
- One thing highly recommended for worship teams is to get an app. As an example, one such app is called OnSong. It's a great program that can be used with iPhone or iPad and completely eliminates sheet music. Another is called Music Stand through Planning Center Online (PCO). Music Stand is an

extension of PCO for once you get on stage. Your needs can be bundled as to what your church wants to develop.

- Along with that, CCLI's Song Select service is an invaluable tool for downloading preformatted songs for your media computer and chord charts for OnSong. OnSong is $25 per device, Song Select is $155/year for smaller churches...but worth every penny!

Chapter 10
The Preaching of the Word

- The general principles of homiletics, rhetoric, and the art of preaching are key fundamentals for setting the atmosphere for the day of worship.
    - It is said, "Practice makes perfect." So, the more you preach, the better you'll become at the art of preaching.
    - You'll develop your own God-given and unique styles as you spend time in God's Word and in the delivery of it.
    - If people don't care for the style of messages, it is likely—in today's postmodern culture— they will not stay long in attendance.
    - Finding a way to reach your audience and knowing your audience is imperative to

growing a healthy church, mentoring, and discipling God's people.

- For the preacher or orator to have studied basic art forms of the various styles of sermons is important for how their audience will receive what they offer in the messages.

> *"Finding a way to reach your audience and knowing your audience is imperative to growing a healthy church, mentoring, and discipling God's people."*

  - o Textual, Topical, Typical, Expository, Biographical, Analytical, Analogical: each offer varying approaches to what or how one ministers their scriptural texts.
  - o Keep in mind, with various tools of stylistic or persuasive approaches learnable, Paul (who was an eloquent speaker, Acts 17) described his preaching as "not with wise or persuasive words, but with a demonstration of the Spirit's power" (1 Cor. 2:4).

Chapter 11
And the Platform

- Water bottles on the platform?
  - Plastic? Blue wrappers? Crunchy noise?
  - How about clear glasses with clear water?
- Kleenex or tissue boxes?
  - Multi-colors? Multi-sizes?
  - How about location? Is it at least symmetrical?
- Cords and wires?
  - Ugh.
- Music stands
  - Ask your worship team to learn the music and prepare visible screens on the back wall for

> "How about clear glasses with clear water?"

their assistance to avoid the music stands and the individuals starring at the sheet music rather than worshipping and leading the people in meaningful and deeply personal worship.

- o Often stands get more in the way than they help, especially for singers.
- Sheet music and books laying on the floor?
- Guitar stands and cases leaned up against the walls or laid on the floors?

Chapter 12
Allowing the Holy Spirit to Engage

- Set the stage. Have you noticed how hard it is for you/us, ourselves, to enter into an atmosphere of "spiritual" and "worship" when we've just come in from grocery shopping, or the ballfield, or a conversation with the lawn mower? Well, think of the people as they walk into church. Then, think of your worship team. They are both the same.
    - Consider having the worship team start worship 15 minutes early; or, have a 30-minute to 1-hour time of prayer, worship, and ministry together, immediately prior to them coming onto the platform to lead worship.

- o Then, the 2-3 songs where they are "warming up" and "not even themselves feeling God's presence really, yet," will be eliminated. As they begin, they will immediately move deeply and much more quickly into the presence of the Lord (because they are "in tune," "prepared," "seasoned," "ready," and already primed for His presence.

> *"Sing more songs to the Lord than about the Lord."*

- o That WILL translate to how quickly and deeply the audience experiences His presence.
- Sing more songs to the Lord than about the Lord.
  - o Immediately drawing people's hearts to worship Him—directly.

> *"Be willing to wait in His presence."*

- Don't rush through the songs.
  - o Purposefully use slow tempos at times, allowing the melodies to penetrate hearts of worshippers.
  - o Don't rush through the services. Lead them there, then allow people time to enter into God's presence.
  - o Be willing to wait in His presence. We can't be in a hurry if we're asking God to come meet with us. It's like saying, "Come meet with us—

bring us Your presence—but, I've only got 60 minutes (for a one-hour service) or 80-90 minutes, including all the peripheral things our service needs (if your service starts at 10:30am, for instance). That would be offensive. Come meet—but do it on my time! I've got to go...

- o So, be willing to let the Holy Spirit lead the service, and be willing to linger and allow the people's worship to linger in His presence—"IF" you reach "His presence" (His inner courts, so to speak).

> *"Let the Holy Spirit lead the service."*

- Focus on the Word of God.
- Work to make sure your worship set is not performance-driven and talent show-operated.
  - o Don't allow the congregants to simply feel they are listening to the singers sing.

    > *"Focus on the Word of God."*

  - o The worship moment is to engage worshippers in adoring and honoring the Lord Jesus Christ at a personal level, not watching, listening, and humming along with the radio.
- Transitions
  - o Distractions do exactly what the word says, distract. Transitions during your service

should be well thought out, planned, and executed to avoid unnecessary distractions.

- After the 5-minute countdown ends, the band begins to play, the lights come up, and the church is greeted. There should never be dead air or dead space unless you are waiting on the Holy Spirit.
- Transitions during worship are successful based on thoughtfulness from one key to the next. If your opening song is in the key of G and your second song in the key of C, think about a middle point. Any worship team should recognize this and realize the first song could go to A or even B in order to transition correctly. Though there is not a perfect science to this, there is the worship of excellence, and hearing a band go from G to C can be excruciating to listen to and ultimately distracting.
- Be sure to meet with your media team and walk through cues, volume settings, and what's on the screen during what times. People are visual, and further, they can hear when something is off. So take the time to eliminate visual and audible distractions.
- Church is successful based off its people and volunteers. So if you need help during a service, let your team know when to come up

before service. It's quite awkward when a preacher clearly isn't ready for something and starts asking for Jim or Bob from the stage or, "Can I get some help down here?" Simply do not do that. Period.

Chapter 13
The Close of the Service: Response and Prayer(s)

- Don't drag it out. We're not more spiritual simply because our worship services are longer. Remember, God can do more in one blink of the eye—a split moment—than man can do in a lifetime.

- Have it worked out in advance for the worship team, or a musician, or "canned music from a CD," or if it is yourself on guitar, piano, or whatever, a certain time on the sermon clock, to have music quietly added to the closing of the sermon.

> *"We're not more spiritual simply because our worship services are longer."*

- Instrumental works best, until a purposed and fitting time for vocals.
- Always give a response moment at the close of each sermon.
  - Or, otherwise called, an altar call.
  - Expect that people have come to the service with heavy hearts and want someone to pray for them; offer the opportunity.
  - Be ready for the Holy Spirit to speak to someone—even if your message was not a salvation message—about giving their lives or rededicating their lives to Christ.
  - Don't shy away from encouraging Water Baptism, soon.
  - Don't shy away from encouraging the Baptism in the Holy Spirit, soon.
- Prayer Teams
  - Some churches have elders or designated prayer teams come to the front to greet/meet people for prayer or to pray with individuals at the altar.
  - If you do that, schedule training for the prayer teams so they'll know what is expected of them and understand how to meaningfully engage, interact with, and pray for others who seek their prayers or counsel.

> *"Always give a response moment at the close of each sermon."*

- o Have resources available for the trained team members to use and to offer to those of whom they may be joining/supporting for prayer.
- Prayer Cloths
  - o Some churches have prayer cloths available to anoint with oil and give to individuals who come to the altar to pray.
  - o If you do this, study prayer cloths; be informed; know what, why, where, when.
  - o Consider having a "stamp" with your church's name and contact info, Scripture verse, etc., stamped on each cloth...or have a ministry group in your church consider embroidering the prayer cloths—and praying over them— before submitting them to the pastor for worship services.
- Several biblical accounts serve as the basis for the modern practice of using a prayer cloth to assist the pray-er to receive positive answers to prayer. Matthew 9:20–22 tells the story of a woman who had suffered severe bleeding for twelve years. She managed to touch the hem of Jesus's cloak, believing this simple contact would heal her. Jesus countered in verse 22, telling her,

> *"Your faith has made you well."* Matthew 9:22 (NLT)

In Matthew 14:34–36, the people of Gennesaret had a similar thought. All the sick from the area desired to touch only the hem of Jesus's garment. All who did were healed. Acts 19:11–12 relates how handkerchiefs that Paul had merely touched were carried to the sick in hopes that people would be healed of diseases and evil spirits.

- o The prayer cloth is a reminder that a group of people are praying for an ailing friend. The group may pray while holding the cloth and then send the cloth to their friend, who keeps it near as a comfort.
- Do you have a bottle of anointing oil anywhere at the platform/altar area for people to provide in anointing individuals, if needed/desired?
  - o Often churches say they believe in it but don't realize they are ill-prepared and haven't added the altar items.
  - o If you do this, study anointing oil; be informed; know what, why, where, when.
- Anointing oil, mentioned 20 times in Scripture, was used in the Old Testament for pouring on the head of the high priest and his descendants and sprinkling the tabernacle and its furnishings to mark them as holy and set apart to the Lord (Exod. 25:6; Lev. 8:30; Num. 4:16). Three times it is called the "holy, anointing oil," and the Israelites were strictly forbidden from reproducing it for personal use

(Exod. 30:32-33). The recipe for anointing oil is found in Exodus 30:23-24; it contained myrrh, cinnamon, and other natural ingredients. There is no indication that the oil or the ingredients had any supernatural power. Rather, the strictness of the guidelines for creating the oil was a test of the obedience of the Israelites and a demonstration of the absolute holiness of God.

Four New Testament passages signify the custom of anointing with oil, and none of them offer a description for its use. We can draw our suppositions from context. In Mark 6:13, the disciples anoint the sick and heal them. In Mark 14:3-9, Mary anoints Jesus's feet as an act of worship. In James 5:14, the church elders anoint the sick with oil for healing. In Hebrews 1:8-9, God says to Christ as He returns triumphantly to heaven, *"Your throne, O God, will last for ever and ever,"* and God anoints Jesus "with the oil of gladness."

- Always have a time of personal prayer during the worship time. This is a time where the pastor/leaders/team offer to anoint people and pray with them for any needs they have (or, people can pray alone at the altar). I've seen an awesome response to this as some people have prayer needs that are unrelated to the sermon or even churches that incorporate weekly communion into this time

Chapter 14
What Are Absolute Impairments to Any Church?

- Dirty facilities
- Non-existent or poor online presence
  - Churches must consider websites and social media presence in today's culture. It's the virtual front door to the church. Most first-time guests in today's global refinement will certainly know all about your church prior to their first arrival. They want to learn about your church before visiting.

> *"Churches must consider websites and social media presence in today's culture. It's the virtual front door to the church."*

  - Instead of having a website, a well-done Facebook page with the right information can be just as effective and more cost efficient! The key is to keep it up to date (I try to post at least once a week).

- o However, churches that only use today's often-seen-as-standard Facebook page can be deemed less professional, less organized, and less prepared for guest arrivals and membership commitments. The mindset of outsiders looking in is often that Facebook pages are for the "insiders" only.

- Immediate change
  - o New pastors and leaders who immediately change things, disengaging from the church's history or past, to solely approach the hopeful future.
  - o While there are times (due to adverse history, usually) that changes need to be made immediately, those are few and rare.

  > "Go slowly.
  > Go slowly.
  > Go slowly."

  - o Go slowly. Go slowly. Go slowly.
  - o Respect the past. Respect former leaders and pastors. Respect the church's history and previous ministries. Respect what God has done previously in His place of worship.
  - o If there is anything of good report, think on these things.
- Members who give them "the look" if they are in "their" seats

- A monotonous and lackluster service or a unscrupulous service
- Insider church lingo—The "AG" will meet at "the Camp" for the "Royal Rangers" event on Saturday.
- Dismal or no signage
- A website that should just "not be"
- No children's church or no nursery
  - Worse: unsafe/unclean/uncomfortable children's church and/or nursery
  - Aloof, distant, perceived as unfriendly people
  - Meet and greet—and few really meeting/greeting them
  - When it's hard to get involved, be connected, become "a part."
  - Without finding "community" or feeling like they fit in, people will leave—quickly.
  - Feeling invisible hurts.
- When the church has cliques
- What about the preaching? Do you ever critique yourself or those filling the pulpit ministry? We should.
- If attendees feel they are not getting anything out of the services, not learning anything
  - Sometimes that's because we don't communicate with clarity.
  - Do we have a clear point to our message(s)?

> *"Without finding "community" or feeling like they fit in, people will leave—quickly."*

59

- Do we use aids, such as (old-fashioned) PowerPoint slides, handouts, or illustrated sermon props?
- Do we use churchy language? I hope not. Speak with a regular voice and use American English (if you're an English-speaking congregation, as would be in my case) like you would on Friday night at a local restaurant. Otherwise, speak your natural dialect of French, Spanish, or whatever it might be.

> *"I'll never forget the first time I personally experienced "feeling" the tangible presence of God in a church service. Trust me, most churches don't offer that, and most of us attending churches do not experience that."*

  - Just don't "turn on" your church voice or your preacher voice. It's not real.
- Do people sense (feel) God's presence in the church services?
  - If not, they'll be detached, apathetic, and superficial in commitment.
    - I'll never forget the first time I personally experienced "feeling" the tangible presence of God in a church

service. Trust me, most churches don't offer that, and most of us attending churches do not experience that. It is a gift. It is a rarity, but doesn't have to be.

- Character failings in church leadership
  - Moral failures
  - Hypocrisy, actual or perceived
  - Lack of consistency in decision making
  - Etc.

Chapter 15
Water Baptism, Baby Dedications, Honorary Events

- Keep "time" in mind; schedule is important, especially if you are in the North American context.
- Have key Scripture written down if needed, or on PowerPoint/screen to assist
- Do you do it "just whenever" or quarterly or...
    - If you do it on a scheduled quarterly basis or something of that nature, then you may have more than one individual/child at a time.
- For baby dedications and baptisms offer a gift (or gifts) such as
    - A Bible
    - Study resources; books

- o Have someone take photos for the families and then print and mail them or email them
  - Get permission before posting on Facebook (varies), especially if children are in the photos.
- o Are there VIP individuals that need to be present or participate?
- o For baptisms, do you provide and keep readily available at all times
  - T-shirts/gowns (for modesty)
    - Some churches provide each person being baptized with a t-shirt, such as "Baptism," "I Have Decided," "Jesus Washed Away My Sin," "All In," or "Made New." Again, you get the picture.
  - Towels
  - Hairdryers
  - And, volunteers for this ministry; if you plan a baptismal, you will need people who will assist the people from start to completion so they have no worries and no issue with changing clothing, hair, etc.
  - One pastor I know drapes a Christian flag around each baptismal candidate as they exit the baptismal.

- Your church may choose another unique idea for making your baptismals special.
- For honorary events, do you offer a special plaque to the person being honored or their family?

Chapter 16
What about Dress Attire?

- Styles have changed in today's culture to a large extent from even 20 years ago. Everything seems to ebb and flow every 25 years or so. But, there are still church cultures that are fairly regimented to their norms.
- What is your church attire culture for your platform?
  - Do you have a dress code?
  - What's appropriate or not appropriate?
    - Whatever your dress code might be, keep it respectful, simple, easily defined, and consistent.

- o It doesn't matter, until … the Sunday you arrive and … it matters. And then it's too late to deal with it at that moment.
  - ▪ The damage done in that instance can be avoided if you'll be proactive and have a plan and a reason, for "who you are" as a church in your vision and culture.

    > "It doesn't matter, until … the Sunday you arrive and … it matters."

  - ▪ Knowing "who you are" will be beneficial for you, your platform team, members, attenders, guests, and the local community at large.

Chapter 17
Service-time Classroom Teachers

- Teachers should always arrive 15-30 minutes earlier than the first student or participants.

> "Teachers should always have an understudy."

- Teachers should always be prepared.
- Teachers should always have an understudy, someone with them as an assistant (when at all possible), to cover little necessities as they would arise and in training to possibly lead, as needed.

Chapter 18
Building Momentum for Ministry Endeavors, Special Offerings, Projects

- A first key is to talk about it often.
- Weave your momentum points into each opportunity to speak to the audience.
  - Sermons
  - Announcements
  - Special prayers
  - Special guests to address topic(s) (like regularly scheduling missionary speakers)

> *"Cancelling scheduled events or services, outings or outreaches, for whatever reasons, discourages congregants and further trains individuals to not trust their own instincts as to when things are announced or scheduled."*

- A second key is to complete what you begin.
  - Cancelling scheduled events or services, outings or outreaches, for whatever reasons, discourages congregants and further trains individuals to not trust their own instincts as to when things are announced or scheduled.
    - They begin wondering if the event will actually occur and thus start opting to not attend, expecting it will not be happening or guessing among themselves whether or not what you've announced is actually going to be.
    - This will most definitely cause a decrease in attendance and in faithfulness among the members, as well as key leaders.

Chapter 19
Small Group Systems

- Has your church developed small group options for attendees to become more relationally involved with ministry, discipleship, and servanthood?
- Keep in mind, small groups should never be an addendum but are ministry and cultural choices made with intentionality.
    - Often churches try to do "a little of this, and a little of that," forgetting the intentionality of the cultural decisions for how they choose to do ministry. It is important to remember, if your church opts for a small-group model, it would be typical consideration that the traditional "Sunday School," midweek Bible

> studies, or previous protocol of these programs would be replaced for the decision of small group systems.
>
> o   If the church tries to do it all, all programs will suffer. So, make your decisions, and work toward those systems for premium effectiveness.

- What demographic options would work for you in your environment?
- Is there a systematic training structure for the leaders, the discussions and group topics, and the scriptural and group dynamics configurations for your small groups?

Chapter 20
Leadership Training Systems

- Has your church developed leadership-training options for staff, for part-time leaders, or for volunteers?
    - And, do you have scheduled events and services on your church calendar to honor leaders, volunteers, and staff?
- What demographic options would work for you in your environment, specifically in the context of leadership development?
- Has your church considered specific development of multi-generational, multi-ethnic, multi-cultural staff, leaders, and ministry volunteers?

Chapter 21
Assimilation Systems

- Do you have a way of tracking weekly and monthly attendance of both regular attenders as well as guests and first-time attendees?
- Consider an Assimilation or Connections Director or Pastor on your staff: volunteer, part-time, or full-time as the case may necessitate.
- Consider community Zone Area Leaders, in various locations around your city and community.

> *"Do you have a way of tracking weekly and monthly attendance of both regular attenders as well as guests and first-time attendees?"*

- Consider in-church Zone Sanctuary Leaders who would oversee certain areas in the sanctuary and be in charge of greeting those in that particular section, meeting newcomers and genuinely caring, praying for, and helping communicate attendee needs and special considerations to the pastor and staff.
- Do you have communication cards?
  - Some churches place these in the pew/chair backs as available opportunities for attendees to communicate prayer requests and other needs to the pastoral staff.
  - And if you do have such cards, do you have a systematic and easy way of using them, receiving them, and following up on them?
- Is there a gift you offer newcomers?
- Does the church offer a newcomer's fellowship or opportunity for new guests and attendees to meet the pastor and staff?
  - I used to offer
    - a quarterly newcomers luncheon,
    - weekly "meet the pastor" opportunities,
    - letters,
    - follow-up from someone within the church other than (me) the pastor,
    - and more.
- Is there a letter or a series of letters, emails, or correspondences that are sent to newcomers, first-

time attenders, and the regular attenders who may have been missing recent services or to whom it has been learned have had mitigating circumstances occurring in their homes?

- Do you provide any training for your Guest Services team members?
- Do you assist newcomers or regular attenders who are not as involved as would be hoped in being introduced to small groups, discipleship groups, or relational connection groups?

> *"Do you have a system of inviting people to join your team?"*

- Do you have a system of inviting people to join your team, offering them ministry responsibilities, service ministries, and options of being a more meaningful part of your leadership or ministry teams?
- Is there a system to offer prayer for your members, your guests, your first-time attenders?
- Is there any suggested invitation and follow-up of one month, quarterly, every six months, or otherwise to those who initially are not networked or connected?

Chapter 22
Missions and Evangelism Systems

- Keep in mind that the structure of how you promote missions may work similarly for other ideas in your church that are more momentum-focused.
  - o Make sure your personal and missional DNA recognizes that missions is not a program. It is the heartbeat of God, the very mandate of Christ.
- When you regularly schedule missionary services/speakers...
  - o The key, initially, is to regularly schedule them.
  - o It is best to not give an honorarium for a missionary; rather, allow the Holy Spirit to

speak to the people and receive a special missions offering for missionary/global workers.

o You'll be surprised as you build upon this concept, how much more income you'll receive for missions, without it affecting your church's tithes and offerings.

> *"It is best to not give an honorarium for a missionary; rather, allow the Holy Spirit to speak to the people and receive a special missions offering for missionary/global workers."*

o Further, by having regular missions speakers, you:

- grow your church's missions awareness, giving, and interests.
- increase the dollars given to missionaries and projects in the USA and around the world.
- build a missional DNA in the hearts of your people.
- cast vision for their callings—as possibly a future missionary will be impacted by your heart and investments.

- o Consider having the missionary speaker in small group environments prior to their speaking in the main worship service event.
- o For example: Sunday School classes, meeting with adults (important), meeting with children (important), meeting with young adults—young married, college age, etc.
- How the pastor should receive an offering for a missionary:
    - o Some missionaries are strong speakers from the pulpit, others not so. While all missionaries have callings used of God, the comfortability of their preaching or receiving of offerings/pledges varies.
    - o Consider, as they complete their presentation/ministry/10-15-minutes window...
    - o The pastor should A) immediately step to the their aid, asking them to remain with them, B) share an encouragement to missionary giving in general and to their ministry specifically, and C) then simply explain to the people, "We have a number of missionary speakers, as we're a missional church. Thank you for giving often above your tithe, for global missions. We're going to receive a special missions offering for _____. If you feel led of the Holy Spirit to assist _____

with this great work, please be obedient to what God is leading you to do. If you gave to a missionary offering last week and simply cannot give this time, no worries at all. We certainly understand. We recognize week to week that some give this week, others next week; some to this missionary, others to that missionary. All we ask is each of us be faithful to whatever the Lord directs us to do. Let's pray..."

- To bring awareness to the missional call of the church, consider using pre-service or during the service
  - 3-minute missions video clips.
  - personal missions testimonials.
  - a weekly (or monthly) prayer for a specific mission/missionary.
  - Speed the Light day, BGMC day, LFTL day, etc. (Each of which are common lingo for my own fellowship, but use what works in your context.)

- Appoint a Missions Board/Missions Committee to oversee missional requests, make decisions, and plan events.
- If your church or fellowship is a part of a denominational or organizational network such as the Assemblies of God, consider an arrangement with church and denominational leaders to offer a

missions pledge to all newly appointed missionaries from your district/network (since they've already been approved and confirmed by the district/network leadership and Assemblies of God World Missions).

- Consider a minimum monthly missions pledge for all AGWM and AGUSM missionaries (if you are a part of the Assemblies of God missions culture).

- Consider a minimum offering for missionary speakers. If the minimum is not reached from the offering received, then the church can increase the offering amount to that minimum (and take what was not received in the offering from the missions account).

- Consider a minimum amount balance to be kept in the missions account for unexpected or miscellaneous expenditures (such as mentioned above, hotels, meals, gifts, as needed, for missionaries).

- And, schedule, plan, and lead regular missions trips and missional opportunities for members both domestically and internationally, in a systematic and regularly scheduled regiment.

- There is no better way of seeing, discipling, and assisting people of God in their heart for missions and outreach than giving the opportunities to do such personally.

- And, keep in mind, if the pastor doesn't lead it, the people will not be given the opportunity to develop in this arena. So, there is great responsibility on pastors and spiritual leaders to help those they are ministering to find their place in the missional callings of Christ.
- All believers are either Senders or Goers. While this could be simplistic in approach, every pastor-leader must recognize the responsibility of developing Christ-followers in their missional giftings.
- Develop evangelism and outreach ministries and offer training.
  - Consider ways to impact local community missional needs: local schools, hospitals, pregnancy centers, homeless centers, food banks, etc.
    - Do your people—members, adherents, leadership team, core leaders—know how to share their personal faith and how to scripturally lead another friend, family member, or co-worker to the Lord?

> *"Call them now to book them for your event two years from now."*

- Always participate in denominational statewide missions projects where multiple churches work together for a greater cause.
- When scheduling keynote missions speakers/leading missionaries as speakers for events/services, keep in mind most keynote-level speakers have schedules

that book one or two years in advance. Call them now to book them for your event two years from now.

- Plan budgetary expenses for transportation, hotels, meals, gift baskets, gifts for the speaker/spouse, and offerings from the church for the speaker/their missions projects.
- When you have a special missionary speaker, consider:
    - Shortening your song selection portion of the service to allow the speaker as much time as possible in the pulpit or for their ministry.
    - Do not schedule on that day unnecessary special announcements, music, presentations, or videos that will use valuable ministry time from the service schedule. The special speaker has come to be with the people that day, and it is the only moment the pastor has to impact the audience with that kind of personal presentation of missions. Allow the speaker as much time as possible.

> *"When you have a special missionary speaker, consider shortening your song selection."*

- Do consider worship songs/music in the service that is missions-focused.

- Do not give an honorarium. Allow the Holy Spirit to speak to the people; receive an offering. If only 5 people are present, the Holy Spirit can speak to one person who can write a check worth hundreds of dollars or more.
    - A first-time attendee (guest) in my church once wrote an $8,000 check to a missionary speaker when I gave the opportunity to respond to the mission's needs. I have often thought to myself, what if I had not given that opportunity? People are altruistic. Give them the opportunity to hear from the Lord. They will often listen and respond.

> *"Encourage altar calls for missions."*

- Find out in advance whether or not the speaker is comfortable—or known from other pastors as being comfortable—with leading the entire sermon. If not, give them a 10-15 minute window.
- Encourage altar calls for missions from among the members/people in the church; opportunities for members of your church to actually respond in saying, I am willing and sensing the call to become a missionary or to become more involved in missions. God calls missionaries from churches just like yours.
- If the missionary is fluent in another language, have them speak/share/pray briefly in that language.

- If the missionary has a family, highlight the family in the service, also.
- Consider having an SS class surprise the family, the children, the spouse, etc., with small gifts that day, while they are with your church.

> "If the missionary is fluent in another language, have them speak/share/pray briefly in that language."

- Consider having an SS class or small group adopt each missionary family that comes with children (whether the church picks them up with a monthly pledge or not) to send them a care package/special offering for Christmas and birthdays. (Or, "adopt" the children by sending them gifts throughout the year. What a way to encourage the missionary moms and dads, by loving and caring for their children!)

> "Do you have a systematic way of training your congregants and members in evangelism?"

- And, do you have a systematic way of training your congregants and members in evangelism? That's what missions is, right? Learning how to do it and sharing one's faith!

Chapter 23
What about Church Planting?

- Have you considered how your church, ministries, and ministry leaders could plant something new across town, in a nearby community, or in an area where you could reach others who might not come to your church or who might not have an opportunity near them to attend a life-giving church?
- Have you considered multi-site church plants for your ministry?
- Have you considered multicultural church plants that could be possible from your ministry?
- Have you considered looking at nearby communities where you could begin an afternoon Bible study in a

home, or a restaurant or coffee shop, in hopes that it could develop into its own church someday?

Chapter 24
The Five-Fold Ministry Gifts

- *"So Christ himself gave the apostles, the prophets, the evangelists, the pastors and teachers"* Ephesians 4:11 (NIV)

- Have you studied them and researched each to understand God's plan for the local church and the nations?

"Are the five-fold gifts functioning in your church and ministries?"

- If a part of an organized church structure or denomination, do they have documentation of this nature that could be to your benefit?

- Are the five-fold gifts functioning in your church and ministries?

- Do you have a plan for training and ministry development in these areas?

Chapter 25
Prayer

- Too many churches and leaders depend on talent and forget the power of prayer.
- Do you spend time praying about your sermon topics before you write them? Before you preach them?
- Do you have prayer teams who pray regularly and systematically for your church, your ministries, your goals, your people?
- Have you considered prayer groups praying during the services while you're preaching?
- Do you have consistent times of prayer with your leadership team(s)?

> *"Too many churches and leaders depend on talent and forget the power of prayer."*

- Are there church leaders who receive congregants and offer prayer for their needs at any moment in your services?

Chapter 26
Social Media

- More than likely, before anyone braves the front entrance of your doors, 9 out of 10 people have looked for you online. Develop a church website, build a church Facebook page, create Twitter and Instagram accounts, and link them all together.

> *"People live on the internet, so give them something to talk about."*

- People live on the internet, so give them something to talk about. Post pictures of the church (pictures you want shown), developments, happy people, people smiling, the next sermon series coming up. Your church will get more chances to grow by simply sharing what God is doing.

- Before people check your church out, they will want to know what they are in for! So put your sermons online through a podcast or Facebook Live. But only do this when you are ready for people to see and hear you.
    - To be honest, a good number of churches use Facebook Live, but they are not yet developed enough to offer excellence to a public audience. And, after all, if we are sharing Jesus, He's worthy of our best!
- Numerous church apps exist already that will allow personalization for your church. Snag a church app for $30 a month and give people the chance to follow you, receive push notifications, download your sermon notes, register for a kids event, join a life group, or give tithes and offerings.

> *"To be honest, a good number of churches use Facebook Live, but they are not yet developed enough to offer excellence to a public audience."*

- I've heard it said that in today's church world over 60% of giving comes from online giving. People live on their phones, and we want to be a part of their lives. But, remember, make it easy, excellent, and exemplary—for Jesus.

Conclusion

So many elements enhance our efforts of presenting Christ and His good news. Certainly, every part of what we do as God-servants should be covered in prayer. God can do more in one blink of the eye than we can do in days, weeks, or months of preparations. Make prayer a priority.

When pastoring a church our leadership developed our missions statement, vision statement, goals, and

> *"We were committed to 1) praise and worship, 2) anointed preaching of the Word, 3) missions, and 4) soul-winning."*

various areas of commitment for our ministries. We were committed to 1) praise and worship, 2) anointed preaching of the Word, 3) missions, and 4) soul-winning. It didn't take me long to realize our four-tiered heartbeat had to be based on some foundational principles: prayer, discipleship, serving, and reproducing/planting. As we strived to meet various aspects of our dreams, we tried our best to stay focused on our committed mission and vision statements.

Let me encourage you to find what you're committed to in the vineyard of God's Kingdom and spend most of your efforts dedicated to fulfilling those things He's called you to do. Churches are unique, individualistic, and divinely designed for select purposes. Honor God. Celebrate your people. And work within your gifts and skillsets to do something amazing for God! He's cheering you on!

> *"Honor God. Celebrate your people. And work within your gifts and skillsets to do something amazing for God! He's cheering you on!"*

Now, begin your lists, the considerations of specifics that can be done to enhance your ministry experiences and services after you've reviewed our chapter discussions:

Review Questions

Now, begin your lists; the considerations of specifics that could be done to enhance your own church's ministry experiences and services after you've reviewed our Chapter Discussions. Remember, you're not trying to compare yourself with the church down the street, or the larger ministry that "has it all", we're merely desiring to honor God with excellence in the things that we can do.

"Remember, you're not trying to compare yourself with the church down the street, or the larger ministry that "has it all", we're merely desiring to honor God with excellence in the things that we can do."

Here are a few questions to help you get started toward making your ministries the best they can be for the Lord. If your church is rural, metropolitan, mobile, inner city, traditional, contemporary, High-Church, or a myriad of alternative options for church start-ups or revitalizations today there are numerous things you can do to shine your brightest and lift Jesus higher.

Don't skip this step. It is the most important step of the book itself. Reading about options offers our heart and minds some considerations that we may have wanted to implement but just haven't gotten around to just yet. Reading reminds us of things we have likely thought of before but have simply put off because of time, budgetary restraints, or various other reasons. But, taking out a pen (or at the least, a pencil to rough out a first draft of thoughts) gives us the opportunity to schedule the changes, make the changes, plan the changes, and cast exciting vision for the church which most always builds momentum, energy, and hopefully synergy for growth. Thinking of all that should be changed, upgraded, enhanced, or whatever (in your context) actually builds excitement and strategic projection for the greatest days your church has ever seen. Enjoy the journey!

Chapter Discussions

Chapter 1: From the Moment People Arrive On the Property

- What opinions or thoughts do you think guests have when they first arrive to your church?

- Is it possible to ask a friend who does not go to church at your church to drive onto the property, even attend a service, to give you a list of written comments and feedback?

- Who are those individuals that you could ask?

- When is the best time for you to have a meeting with key leaders and members to discuss with them the matters you've learned in this book? Schedule that.

- If you created a list of items / needs that is on the vision list to enhance, where could you print that, offer that, give that out to individuals to see if they'd consider taking care of the expense(s) of one or more of the items for the church?

- Are there neighboring churches that would Reach Up, Reach Down, or Reach Across to help our church? Make the list of who to call to meet with personally to discuss these things.

Chapter 2: As People Walk Into the Church

- If the entry way and first impression inside the door offers a less than welcoming environment, what can be immediately done to remedy all or some of it?

- What would it take for me to add music playing in hallways, entryway, and parking lot(s)?

- Are our churches door greeters suited for the job?

- More than simply my greeters, whom can I enlist to be helpers at the doors, give tours, or to walk with people to the nursery or children's areas if needed?

- What multi-generational ministries could make a difference for our church?

- What church can I visit simply to see how they do signage in their church hallways?

- What day on your calendar will you block out some time to take a simple survey to register your church and begin the journey of being a Disability Friendly Church? Go to: http://www.specialtouch.org/leadership.

- How can our church's Welcome Center be enhanced?

Chapter 3: Waiting for the Service to Begin

- Do I need to have a training session with my sound booth personnel to help them be more scheduled, timed, accommodating with fade-downs, fade-ups, microphones ON, microphones OFF, etc.?

- What can be done to bring calm to the sanctuary atmosphere at least thirty minutes prior to a service?

- Would it help our church to begin using a count-down clock on the screen(s)?

- What list of faithful members can be enlisted as Section Greeters?

- Is it time to bury the printed bulletin?

- What missionaries/global workers can I begin highlighting as a Missionary of the Month?

Chapter 4: Are My Children Safe?

- What children's ministries or teen ministries workers in my church are being used but are yet to have completed back-ground checks?

- What training should I be offering for the volunteers, staff, or church leadership?

- When will I implement a security check-in system for the children's ministries and nursery?

Chapter 5: Are People Mingling and Milling Around?

- Are there cliques in our church that are alienating certain individuals?

- If so, what are areas that could be offered to develop relationships among groups that would not normally interact?

- Has there ever been an all-church members training on how we can be more guest friendly and welcoming?

- When can it be scheduled?

Chapter 6: Stewardship: Receiving Tithes and Offerings

- What twelve lessons (one per month) (at a minimum) can be developed as a 2-minute comment just before tithes and offerings are mentioned and received from the congregants?

- Is there music being played underneath the offering prayers?

- If our church uses the same person(s) regularly (typically board members or key leaders) to come up and pray over the tithes and offerings, are their backs to the audience when they pray?

- Can I pass a microphone to them, at least, for their prayer?

Chapter 7: Special Announcements or Presentations

- What can specifically be added to our services that can be a statement or significant welcome for first-time guests or those not accustomed to our traditions?

- Do I have marked in my bible the key verses related to communion, tongues, and gifts of the Spirit so I can specifically read a brief passage of scripture when those occurrences are offered in our services? (It so helps guests, especially, but also long-term members, to see their pastor walk to the podium and open the bible to encourage them in the various ways the Lord is working in their midst.)

Chapter 8: Taking Care of Guest Speakers

- In what further ways can our church honor guest speakers or guests to our worship services?

- Could I possibly create a rotation of key church leaders to be guest hosts?

- What names could I place on that list?

Chapter 9: The Worship Team

- Do I need to first have a meeting with just my worship leader (and/or them and their spouse, if applicable) to explain what I want to do and how I'm hoping to see them do what I'm expecting?

- What new individuals can be added to our church worship ministries?

- Should I consider a similar conversation about our church platform dress attire?

- If worship team practice is obstructing main worship schedules, classes, etc., what day and time could be offered to re-schedule the practices?

Chapter 10: The Preaching of the Word

- What can I do to become a better preacher of the Word?

- Is there a conference, class, or training venue that I could attend?

- Are there certain podcasts, ministers, or mentors that I could learn and glean from?

Chapter 11: The Platform

- What are the aesthetic issues that I see on our platform?

- How can our church better tidy up the platform area?

- Would it be possible for our worship team singers to memorize the words?

- Should I consider a pastor's seat on the platform? Or, not? And, why? (Do what works best for your context.)

Chapter 12: Does the Holy Spirit Engage Our Worship to Impact Lives?

- How difficult would it be for our worship team to begin 10-15 minutes prior to the worship start time?

- Of a typical music worship set from our worship team, are there songs that can be eliminated to more readily and quickly move the service to genuine worship?

- Could we sing more songs "to the Lord" than "about the Lord"?

- How can I, as pastor, offer insights and training to our worship leader(s) on not rushing things, slowing tempos, and genuinely leading people into personal worship?

Chapter 13: The Close of the Service; Response & Prayers

- Should our services (based on culture) consider a more time conscious schedule for the worship services?

- Have I considered a set time on the clock as the minister/pastor is still preaching, a musician comes to the platform and begins to play to assist in the transition to close, rather than publicly calling musicians forward?

- Have I been slack in giving altar calls or response moments?

- How can I better that element of our services?

- Do we offer a time of personal prayers for congregants to be prayed for?

Chapter 14: What Are Absolute Impairments to Any Church?

- When is the last time the church board or elders did a walk through the facilities with pen and paper writing down any structural issue, un-kept spots, dirty / needing cleaned locations, painting needs, etc.?

- If we do not yet have a meaningful web and social media presence who in our church can assist us with creating one?

- If I (pastor) am fairly new (especially one year or less) what are things that I want to do immediately that I should slow down with and approach more cautiously?

- What are ways that our church can give honor to the past?

- How can I communicate better in every area of the ministry?

- And, who can assist me with those enhanced communications?

Chapter 15: Water Baptisms, Baby Dedications, Honorary Events, etc.

- Who can I (the church leadership) enlist to be a key volunteer in helping make these ministry moments meaningful and run smoothly?

- What individual(s) in our church can assist with photography for major events such as these?

- Do I need to order baptismal and dedicatory gifts, t-shirts, or materials?

Chapter 16: Dress Attire?

- What would be appropriate dress attire for our church?

- What dress attire would be considered inappropriate?

- Do I have this information in written context anywhere?

Chapter 17: What about Classroom Teachers?

- Do we allow each teacher or small group leader to set their own teaching materials?

- Should I be considering a standardized curriculum (from one's denomination) or materials that follow along with the pastor's sermons, etc.?

- Are there teachers and class leaders that I need to address problem areas to be considered or changed?

Chapter 18: Building Momentum for Ministry Endeavors, Missions, Special Projects

- What are ways I can be reminded to mention and talk about key momentum points weekly and/or regularly?

- Who can you utilize to review your sermons in advance giving them freedom to add in bullet points that come to their mind, which you may have forgotten or not thought of?

- Have I/we been in a habit of canceling services or not keeping a standard published schedule?

- Should I consider ways to encourage the members and congregants who may have been discouraged by inconsistency?

- If attendance has seemingly decreased, do I have a plan of assimilation for members and guests to

123

contact them and encourage, edify, strengthen, and build relationships?

Chapter 19: Small Group Systems

- Are we intentional about small groups?

- Or, is our church using small groups as an addendum and not really seeing momentum from them?

- What are key demographic groups in our church or community that we should target for small groups?

- Do I offer training for leaders?

Chapter 20: Leadership Training Systems

- Could I begin using on-line training materials offered from My Healthy Church, RightNow Media, Tom Rainer, The Family Foundation, Dick Hardy, Engage Media, Exponential, CMN, etc.?

- What specific changes or enhancements can be made to assist my group teachers in systematic structures, discussion topics, or in the how-to of doing their groups?

Chapter 21: Assimilation Systems

- When will I begin a system of tracking attendance?

- Who in our church can oversee this assimilation ministry?

- What members of our church could be appointed as assimilation deacons (use the verbiage best for your culture)?

- How many Sections within our church sanctuary would need a Section Leader?

- How many Zones of our community would we target with a Zone leader?

- Who can develop communication cards for our church?

- And, who will be in charge of picking those up weekly, and documenting the information to be presented in a timely fashion to pastor and/or leadership?

Chapter 22: Missions & Evangelism Systems

- How many global workers / missionaries are scheduled for this year to visit and minister (or do a window) in our church?

- Can we in faith add one per month?

- What can I do as pastor to build a missions DNA in our church?

- Have my spouse (if applicable) and I, as pastors, been on a missions trip?

- Can we schedule and plan a missions trip for members of our church, either in the USA or cross-culturally in another country?

- Have I (pastor and church board) chosen a minimum financial gift to give missionaries? (Of course, there is never a maximum gift. Whatever is received in a

129

missionary offering should be given to the missionary and their work.)

Chapter 23: What about Church Planting?

- How can we set vision to multiply ourselves for the Kingdom?

- Is there a multi-cultural opportunity for your church?

- Are there ethnicities that your church could assist with beginning a bible study group or new church plant for their own language demographics?

Chapter 24: The Five-Fold Ministry Gifts

- Which of the five-fold ministry gifts are regularly functioning in your church?

- Which of the five-fold ministry gifts are not seemingly functioning in your church?

- How can you, as pastor/leader, develop members to use their gifts for the Lord and His work?

Chapter 25: Prayer

- Has our church been too focused on talent and found ourselves missing in the area of prayer?

- When is the best time for me, as pastor, to spend time praying about my sermons and sermon topics?

- What can be done to develop prayer teams who pray regularly and systematically for our church, our ministries, our goals, our people, etc.?

- Would it be a good idea to consider prayer groups praying during the services, during the preaching?

- When can the pastor and leadership genuinely spend time in prayer together?

- Are there church leaders who receive congregants and offer prayer for their needs at any moment in your services?

- What other prayer ministries could be added to our church?

Chapter 26: Social Media

- Have you ever conducted a survey sample of the number of people in your church that looked for your church online before attending?

- If your church has a website, does it need to be updated?

- How often is your church social media updated?

- Who in your church could oversee Social Media?

- What is happening in your church that you wish the community were informed?

- If our church does Facebook Live, does it give a positive representation of what we want to share publicly with the community?

- Why? Why not?

    - Should our church consider an app?

- Should we enhance our giving options through social media?

About Joseph S. Girdler, D.Min

Superintendent, Kentucky
Assemblies of God (USA)

Education

University of Kentucky, 1984
        BA, Psychology
        BA, Communications

Asbury Theological Seminary, 1991
        MA, Missions & Evangelism

Evangel University / Assemblies of God Theological Seminary, 2018
        D.Min

Married

Pastor Joe married Renee (Dr. Renee Vannucci Girdler) on June 7, 1986. Renee is the daughter of Assemblies of God pastors from eastern Kentucky. Both parents were 100% Italian, with grandparents on both sides of her family migrating to the United States from Italy in the 1930s.

Having served as chief resident in Family Medicine and graduating from the University of Kentucky Medical School with honors, Renee is a board-certified family medicine physician with Norton Healthcare Systems in Louisville. She is the former clinic director and vice chair of the Department of Family Medicine at the University of Louisville, as well as the former director of Clinical Affairs and vice chair of the Department of Family Medicine at the University of Kentucky. Her specialties include Women's Health Care and Diabetes, while having further interactions, as well, with International Medicine.

With an extensive background in ministry, she was previously honored by the former general superintendent of the Assemblies of God, Dr. Thomas Trask, and former AG World Missions director, John Bueno, by her selection as the first female in Assemblies of God history appointed to the World Missions Board of the Assemblies of God. She was honored by former general superintendent, Dr. George O. Wood, in receiving the General Superintendent's Medal of Honor, the Fellowship's highest honor for lay individuals in the Assemblies of God (received at General Council 2011, Phoenix, Arizona). Renee was a longtime member of the Board of Directors for Central Bible College and Evangel University. Renee's medical and missions travels/ministries have included Ecuador, Peru, Argentina, France, Spain, Mexico, South Africa, and Belgium.

Personal

- Born: Corbin, Kentucky, June 7, 1962
- High School: Laurel County High School, London, Kentucky. President of Beta Club, 2-year inductee to the Kentucky All-State Concert and Symphonic Bands
- College: Graduate of the University of Kentucky, 1980–1984; 4-year Music Scholarship recipient (trpt), President UK Band, Vice-President Psi Chi, Mortar Board
- Married: Dr. Renee V. Girdler, 1986
- Children: Steven Joseph Girdler, MD, born 1991 (wife, Julia). Steven is a physician at Mt. Sinai Medical Center, New York, NY, Orthopedic Surgery.
- Children: Rachel Renee Girdler, MSW, born 1995. Rachel is a missionary associate, Ecuador.

Ministry

- Ordained: Assemblies of God, Kentucky District Council, 1994
- Superintendent: Kentucky Assemblies of God, 2004–Present
- General Presbyter: Assemblies of God USA, 2004–Present
- District Missions Director: Kentucky Assemblies of

God, 1997–2005
- Senior/Lead Pastor: King's Way Assembly of God, Versailles, Kentucky, 1992–2004
- Associate Pastor, Music, Youth: King's Way Assembly of God, Versailles, Kentucky, 1988–1992
- Chi-Alpha College Campus Associates: Morehead State University, Morehead, Kentucky, 1987–1988

Being raised Southern Baptist and Missionary Baptist, and then attending a primarily Methodist seminary, "Pastor Joe" began ministry serving the college campus of Morehead State University in Morehead, KY, with the Assemblies of God. Followed by four years of music ministry and youth ministry, he was propelled to a lead pastorate in 1992. His welcoming relationships with pastors of multiple fellowships and denominations have served him well in developing a broad and ecumenical approach to church networks globally. Early in ministry he was asked to serve in state-wide denominational leadership. Serving initially as the Kentucky Assemblies of God World Missions director for 7 years while simultaneously pastoring King's Way Assembly in the Lexington, KY, area for a total of 16 years, Pastor Joe was then elected as the Kentucky Assemblies of God district superintendent in 2004.

Initially a revitalization project, his pastorate with the King's Way congregation found the church overcoming paramount obstacles from the onset, but then underwent three building programs and grew to an average attendance of 400+ people. A key element was that the church grew their missional stewardship from about $15,000 to an annual missions giving of over $430,000 in only 12 years. The last year of his pastorate ('03) the church attained more than $1,000 per person, per capita missions giving, over and above the church's regular tithes and offerings. The church was honored, of well over 12,000 Assemblies of God USA congregations at that time, to achieve Top 100 status in Assemblies of God World Missions giving. Their ministry site by that time of almost 40 acres and assets of approximately $4 to $5 million at the time of his transition had become one of the strongest Assemblies of God congregations in the Kentucky Assemblies of God, baptizing new converts during the morning worship service nearly every Sunday. The church's academic childcare ministry (King's Way Academy) was at the time one of the largest in the region with over 150 children five days per week and a full-time staff of over 25 leaders.

Drs. Joseph and Renee Girdler both serve (present and previous) on numerous boards and committees throughout the Assemblies of God fellowship. Their unique journey of together integrating both ministry and medicine has offered numerous opportunities to encourage next-generational leadership in the callings of God. Of many global travels, his missions ministries have included Argentina, Peru, Ecuador (20+ times), Mexico, El Salvador, Brazil, Italy, Germany,

Austria, Spain, France, Belgium, England, Turkey, Bulgaria, and more.

Contact Information:
Email: jsgirdler@kyag.org
Office: (502) 241-7111
Website: www.kyag.org
P.O. Box 98
Crestwood, KY 40014, USA